Harold Pinter

by WALTER KERR

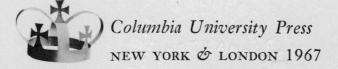

Columbia University Press
NEW YORK *&* LONDON 1967

COLUMBIA ESSAYS ON MODERN WRITERS is a series of critical studies of English, Continental, and other writers whose works are of contemporary artistic and intellectual significance.

Editor: William York Tindall

Advisory Editors

Jacques Barzun   W. T. H. Jackson   Joseph A. Mazzeo   Justin O'Brien

Harold Pinter is Number 27 of the series

WALTER KERR is Sunday drama critic for *The New York Times*.

PN
1707
K4

Acknowledgment is made to *The Paris Review* and to the Viking Press Inc., for quotations from the Harold Pinter Interview by Lawrence Bensky.

Acknowledgment is made also to Grove Press, Inc., and to Methuen & Company Ltd. for quotations from the plays of Harold Pinter. A listing of the plays and their dates of copyright appears in the Bibliographical Note to this pamphlet.

Harold Pinter

Harold Pinter seems to me the only man working in the theater today who writes existentialist plays existentially. By this I mean that he does not simply content himself with restating a handful of existentialist themes inside familiar forms of playmaking. He remakes the play altogether so that it will function according to existentialist principle.

To show this it will be necessary to recapitulate briefly, and at the expense of some subtlety, the premises on which existentialist philosophy rests. At root, existentialism rejects the ancient Platonic principle that essence precedes existence.

What does this mean, practically speaking? Platonic theory, made more explicit by Aristotle and then accepted as a habit of thought by Western society in succeeding generations, proposed that before any one man, say, came into being there had to exist, somewhere in the mind of the universe, an idea of man—an immaterial essence which contained, bounded, dictated the nature of the species.

In this view, the essence Man exists before any one individual man. Individual men are, in effect, derived from it. They take their physical, mental, and moral capacities from it. Because individual men are concrete, idiosyncratic, and limited by having been incorporated in matter, no one of them perfectly expresses or realizes the abstract universal from which he has taken his name and shape. Pure being—including the pure essence "man"—is a sort of fountainhead, a reservoir, a pool of unadulterated spirit from which isolated individuals siphon off

[3]

so much spirit as they have. Aristotle located this immaterial and universalized source in the mind of God. God thereafter, as it were, made man by die-stamp. From the concept "man," men took their existence. Existence became a hand-me-down. Men, as they walked the earth, were predefined. They conformed to an essence prior to themselves.

Viewed in a Platonic light, man was both inhibited and most helpfully guided. He was inhibited in the sense that he could not escape the boundaries set for him by his essential nature. Though he was obviously in some measure free, he was not free to behave as other than a man—and what a man was could be explicitly determined. Man was made to perform in a certain way, to pursue certain goals, to expect certain natural and logical rewards and punishments depending upon how well or ill he played out his assigned role.

The inhibition had its comforts. If man was predefined, he did have an identity. He was this, not that. He had a name, an address, a secure position in the universe. He was not altogether footloose in a void, he had instincts, a conscience, and an intelligence to tell him what steps to take. These tools were trustworthy precisely because they belonged to, or were drawn from, the essence "man." Listened to, or used properly, they could not very well lie. What was Of The Essence was bound to return to the essence, to echo it, to reflect it as a mirror reflects. Man could know himself by drawing deductions from the equipment he had been given.

Existentialist philosophy, moving from troubled speculation in the nineteenth century to aggressive assertion in the twentieth, reverses the Platonic order. It insists that existence precedes essence. That is to say, the notion of an original, immaterial archetype is jettisoned. There is no matrix from which individual men in the concrete are drawn. There are only individual men, born undefined. It is not even possible to say what a "man" is until we have seen how this man or that man actually behaves, until we see what this man or that man has done. Man does not come to the planet with an identity; he spends his time on the planet arriving at an identity.

As with the Platonic view, this new insistence has its comforts and its cruelties. Its principal comfort, which may in the first stages of discovery seem small comfort, lies in the unprecedented freedom now granted to man. Man is no longer to regard himself as confined by a "nature," by a given set of behavior patterns which are inbred and fundamentally inviolable. He is open, an experiment, a reaching, an adventure. There are no known limits to his possible activity. Man has no absolute face to be worn daily and Sunday; he can make as many faces as he likes, in something of the manner that Albert Camus' Caligula does.

At the same time he must walk through the world alone, without instructions from a central computer, without friends who share his nature, without confidence that his intelligence reflects anything absolute, without assurance that he fits into any discernible scheme. He is nameless, as yet featureless; he *is* footloose in a void; and his task, if he can be said to have one, is to create his identity by exercising his freedom to act. When he has done all that he can do, he may be able to say what *he* is. He may achieve his essence. Until the ultimate moment of actualization comes, however, he must move, with some vertigo, through a silent universe. Man is "condemned" to be free, Sartre says.

From these various corollaries of the proposition that existence precedes essence have come the characteristic dramatic themes of our time. Who am I? the man asks as he discovers that he has lost the wallet that contained his identity cards. Why can't we communicate? the stranger on the park bench snarls. Why has man no home? the vast, vacant settings on a hundred stages inquire. What are reasoning, logic, intelligence worth? demand the professors who contradict themselves word by word, line by line. What are we waiting for? wonder the nonentities who have been waiting so long for Godot. Is anything real or is everything illusion? anguish all of the people who cannot find themselves in mirrors. How silly conformity is when there is no essence to conform to!

Dozens of playwrights have made use of existentialist themes. What is surprising is that none of them—none but Harold Pinter, I think—has taken the fundamental proposition seriously enough to present his plays in the new existentialist sequence. Whether Mr. Pinter would wish to call himself a formal existentialist, or whether he has taken a creative leap intuitively, I do not know. Playwrights are properly wary of labeling themselves, and it is in any case more important to know what plays do than what playwrights say they are meant to do. The philosophical impulse has, however, been the dominant experimental impulse during the time Pinter has been at work; Pinter is reported by Ronald Bryden as having been profoundly influenced by *Waiting for Godot* the year before he began his first plays; and the playwright's occasional remarks to interviewers, which we shall have to attend to shortly, strongly suggest that his rejection of Platonic sequence has been as deliberate in intention as it has been unique in practice.

In the current philosophical climate, the matter of sequence should be important. If existence does indeed precede essence, if an actual thing precedes an abstract concept of that thing, then it should also do so on the stage. Exploratory movement in the void, without preconception or precommitment, should come first. Conceptualization should come later, if at all.

But Samuel Beckett, for instance, does not really work that way. Mr. Beckett has been most influential in imposing upon contemporary theatergoers an awareness of existential loneliness, homelessness, facelessness; our strongest image of the void comes from the careful emptiness of his plays. Yet Mr. Beckett takes his curtain up upon a woman buried waist-deep in sand. Or upon an aged couple confined to ashbins. Or upon Didi and Gogo immobilized, already waiting.

The fact that Mr. Beckett does not make much use of the existentialist freedom to act is not the point here. A playwright is free to use one strand of available material to the exclusion of others; he is a temperament, not necessarily a doctor of philosophy. The point is that in each case—in all cases where Beckett is concerned, I would say—we are first offered a concept, a statement of essence. What the opening image of *Happy Days* says to us, immediately, is that man is essentially earthbound. Nagg and Nell in *Endgame*, lifting the lids of their ashbins occasionally but never leaving them, are essentially discards. In *Waiting for Godot* Lucky is seen as essential slave, Pozzo as essential master.

Lucky and Pozzo are not open, undefined figures who become slave and master, who arrive at their natures through exploratory action in the void. They appear fully formed, samples from their respective matrices: Pozzo with a rope, Lucky bearing a heavy load. Whatever Mr. Beckett's philosophical disposition may be, he builds plays as a Platonist. He forms an abstract concept of man's nature and role and presents it to us in its original conceptual form, individualizing it only very slightly. We are not concerned with persons forming themselves; we are concerned with persons inhabiting set forms they cannot escape.

Our habits of thought are so strong—after several thousand years of being trained in Greek method—that even when we wish to make an anti-conceptual statement, even when we wish to say that man has not been and cannot be defined, we do it by conceptualization, by starting from a definition. First we reach a conclusion, perhaps the conclusion that logic is a meaningless tool. Then we arrange a stage illustration to show that it is meaningless, as Ionesco does in *Rhinoceros:*

"The cat has four paws. Isidore and Fricot both have four paws. Therefore Isidore and Fricot are cats."

"My dog has got four paws."

"Then it's a cat."

Or perhaps we have reached the conclusion that words are essentially without valid content and that therefore communication by language is essentially illusory. Ionesco again, this time in *The Bald Soprano:*

"I've never seen her. Is she pretty?"

"She has regular features and yet one cannot say that she is pretty. She is too big and stout. Her features are not regular but still one can say that she is very pretty. She is a little too small and too thin."

These last cancellations—in which "too small and too thin" directly contradict "too big and stout"—are of course deliberately devised by the playwright in order to demonstrate an idea about the futility of verbal communication. There is no testing toward discovery. The playwright has reached his conclusion before beginning to write, and then has measured his illustration exactly to display that conclusion—precisely as another playwright might begin with the essential quality of Ambition and then manufacture a character to conform to it. Though Samuel Beckett holds very little in common with the medieval world-view of things, his actual method of composition is not radically different from that of the author of *Everyman.* A symbol—which is the sign of an essence—is hung up in plain view; later, some individualizing detail is added to it, though not so much as to obscure its continuing function as an abstract, almost immaterialized, concept.

Thus, though the drained-out and disjointed worlds which Beckett, Ionesco, and other contemporary playwrights place upon the stage may at first sight seem very strange indeed, the strangeness consists almost entirely in what is being said, in the inverted value-system that is carefully organized into an image. There is very little that is strange in the organizing process itself. The Platonic sequence keeps its grip on us: a concept precedes, and dominates, whatever we see existing on the stage.

"I don't conceptualize in any way," Pinter has said in an interview given to Lawrence M. Bensky for *Paris Review*, a statement which may well be taken at face value and which may help to explain why Pinter's plays seem strange to us through and through.

Watching a Beckett play, we immediately engage in a little game of "Concept, concept, who's got the concept?", no doubt because we sense that, beyond the play's opaque surface, there lies a conceptual nub. We want to get at this, to abstract it. We know that it was abstract to begin with.

Watching a Pinter play, we give over the scramble to stick pins in ideas and fix them forever to a drawing-board. We feel that the drawing-board isn't there and that our eager thumbs would only go through it. Instead of trying to bring matters to a halt by defining them, we permit them to move at will, understanding that we have been promised no terminal point. We give existence free rein, accept it as primary, refrain from demanding that it answer our questions, grant it the mystery of not yet having named itself.

To have drawn us into so complete a surrender of our ordinary, long-standing expectations and demands is a considerable achievement, and Mr. Pinter has taught us to follow the sequence his way by being strict in his presentation of it.

To begin with the matter of place. In his very first play, *The*

Room, written in 1957, the existentialist challenge is formidable—and, within the limited confines of the piece, absolutely met.

Existentialism imagines man living in a void. At the same time it asks that we refrain from conceptualizing this void. How shall it be defined when it has not yet been fully explored? In short, we are asked to enter a void that is not an abstract void.

The Room completely satisfies this difficult—one would have thought impossible—requirement. Everything in "a room in a large house" is entirely tangible, concrete, present not as idea but as actuality. There is a gas-fire, a perfectly real one. A gas-stove and sink. A window. Table and chairs. A rocking chair. The foot of a double bed protruding from an alcove. The walls are solid, the dirty wallpaper has been firmly pasted up, the objects handled by a slatternly housewife as she moves in and about the aggressively dimensional furniture all have weight, texture, the density of experienced life.

These objects, and the actions involved in handling them, are given blunt importance in the stage directions—not as symbols of other values but in and for themselves. They are important because they are there, because they exist. Handling them is important because they are there to be handled, and because hands exist.

Rose is at the stove. . . . She places bacon and eggs on a plate, turns off the gas and takes the plate to the table. . . . She returns to the stove and pours water from the kettle into the teapot, turns off the gas and brings the teapot to the table, pours salt and sauce on the plate and cuts two slices of bread. . . . She butters the bread. . . . She goes to the sink, wipes a cup and saucer and brings them to the table. . . . She pours milk into the cup. . . . Sits in the rocking-chair.

There is no comment in all of this, no suggestion that plate or teapot, salt or sauce, contains a meaning that will serve as metaphor for some larger value. The salt does not represent savor, or the loss of it; it is salt. The sauce is not poisoned, nor does the housewife's action in serving it signify the slavery of Woman. The rocking-chair does not mean to suggest that Rose has retired from life, or is a lulled prisoner of it. We are to attend to these things as things. The deliberateness, the patience, the concentration with which these companions in existence are listed and then handled breeds a kind of awed respect for them. Audiences tend to stare at the cup, at the stove, at the chair with an unfamiliar intensity. Each object seems more important than it would in another kind of play precisely because it is not a minor sign, a diminutive stand-in, for something of greater significance than itself but because all of the significance it has is its own. Everything that exists is self-contained. It does not derive from something prior to it, nor is it a marker indicating something to come. It *is* now. Handle with care.

Objects observed in a Pinter play tend to generate something like awe. They may be utterly commonplace, they usually are; yet they seem uncommon here because they have not been absorbed into a pattern that explains them away as mere tools of a narrative or as looming symbols of conceptual value. Sometimes these objects acquire such self-importance as to seem ominous, though that is not their initial function in a Pinter play. If we feel faintly startled to see how solid a cup is, or how shaped, we feel so—in the beginning—only because we are used to ignoring the solidity and shape of cups in our absent-minded lives. Normally we think of a cup as a means to an end, as an indifferent utility making a passing contribution to another, much more identifiable, purpose: our tea, our pleasure, our life-roles as wife, husband, host. Thinking of a cup in this way, we render it more or less invisible. In effect, we make it absent.

By suppressing the past and future of the cup, by refusing to name its origin or its destiny, Pinter increases its presence. It catches, and for the moment wholly occupies, our eye.

Whatever exists in the room is made to exist at its maximum intensity. Nothing within our view is in any way abstract, as, say, the landscape of *Waiting for Godot* is abstract. *Waiting for Godot* takes place Nowhere, or Anywhere. But in *The Room* we are Somewhere. Environment is utterly explicit; every piece on the premises could be sold at auction, the place as a whole could be rented.

At the same time that the tangible is insisted upon, literally thrust into our faces, the surrounding void is implied. The void is outside the room, upstairs, downstairs, everywhere beyond the walls. The real is real. The void envelops it. It is all rather as though a cyclone had picked up a still intact shed—as we used to see cyclones do in the movies—and were carrying it, still intact, through unknown air to an unknown end.

The outlying void is rhythmically described as Rose rocks. Does anyone live below Rose and her husband, in the basement? "I don't know who lives down there now. . . . I think there was one first, before he moved out. Maybe they've got two now."

Perhaps there's no one below. No matter. "If they ever ask you, Bert, I'm quite happy where I am. We're quiet, all right. You're happy up here. It's not far up either, when you come in from outside. And we're not bothered. And nobody bothers us."

Upstairs may be empty, too. When Mr. Kidd, the landlord, drops by, Rose asks him "Anyone live up there?"

"Up there?" Mr. Kidd ponders. "There was. Gone now."

"How many floors you got in this house?

"Floors. . . . Ah, we had a good few of them in the old days."

"How many have you got now?"

"Well, to tell you the truth, I don't count them now."

"Oh."

"No, not now."

Though the immediate room, the direct experience of life, is entirely dimensional, the universe in which it exists is unstructured. There is not even any knowing where Mr. Kidd lives, once he leaves these tight, tangible four walls. A prospective tenant asks Rose where the landlord might be:

"Well, say I wanted to get hold of him, where would I find him?"

"Well,—I'm not sure."

"He lives here, does he?"

"Yes, but I don't know—"

"You don't know exactly where he hangs out?"

"No, not exactly."

"But he does live here, doesn't he?"

" . . . As a matter of fact, I don't know him at all. We're very quiet. We keep ourselves to ourselves. I never interfere. I mean, why should I? We've got our room. We don't bother anyone else. That's the way it should be."

Rose, who is only Rose and not Everyman, knows only what she experiences: her husband drives a van and enters and leaves the room at regular hours; a landlord drops in, but lives no defined existence once he has left; it is dark outside; it is cold inside; sitting down and getting up are important matters because they are events which truly happen as opposed to the mere rumor of events beyond the room; cups and saucepans can be touched.

Whatever impinges directly upon the consciousness is the sum total of what can be known. We share Rose's consciousness, knowing exactly as much as she does and no more.

Let alone, Rose would be content simply to exist.

Rose is not let alone, any more than the two hired killers in *The Dumb Waiter* are let alone. Quite soon Rose is disturbed by two discoveries. Apparently it is her room that is to let. Though the rest of the "building" may very well be unoccupied, the prospective tenants may be in the act of displacing her. And it would seem that someone does indeed live in the basement, someone who may intrude upon her at any moment.

As we move from the solid-inside-a-void environment of a Pinter play toward what we shall have to call the narrative movement of the people who have their being in that environment, we are instantly embroiled in threat. "Menacing" is the adjective most often used to describe the events in a Pinter play, "suspense" is considered one of the playwright's most satisfying effects.

It is almost shocking that this should be so. For narrative suspense in the past has almost always been derived from one clear source: known danger. Oedipus' fears are absolutely defined: the tyrant lives in dread that somewhere, somehow, it shall be proved that he has killed his father and married his mother. If Oedipus tries to blot these things from his mind, it is because they are so terribly present to his mind. Macbeth knows that it is Macduff he has to fear; no matter how much certain prophecies seem to support the notion that Macduff cannot be the man to best him, Macbeth trembles in apprehension. Willy Loman worries that he will not be liked. Charlie Chaplin worries that the cabin in which he is trapped will tumble over a precipice before he can get out of it. Watching these figures, we are frightened for them because we see—we are able to name and describe—the shape of the terror advancing upon them.

Yet the one thing Mr. Pinter steadfastly refuses to do is to offer his audience—or his characters—any information whatsoever about the forces they come to feel as hostile. We see no precipice; we are not told what may happen at the stroke of midnight; no oracle spells out, not even in ambiguous terms, the doom to be looked for. Ordinarily, danger is conceived in the future tense: this is what will happen if steps are not taken to avoid it. Apprehension rises as the future comes closer—while still remaining the future. Mr. Pinter writes exclusively in the present tense.

In *The Dumb Waiter*, written during the same year as *The Room*, two minor-league thugs are uneasily whiling away the time in a basement room. Presumably they have been sent there to do a killing. They do not know, however, who is to be killed. Neither do they seem to know who has hired them. This is simply the situation in which they find themselves: it is without an explicit beginning, it looks forward to no explicit end. Once again the situation itself—everything that belongs to the experienced moment—is concrete. There are newspapers to be read, lavatories to be flushed, biscuits to be parceled out, gas-ranges to be lighted.

After they have waited a while, sometimes quarrelling over football matches and tea, an overlooked dumb-waiter in the wall gives off a sudden clatter. Opening the slot, the two men discover that an order for food has been sent down. "Two braised steaks and chips. Two sago puddings. Two teas without sugar," the order reads. But though the order itself is once again explicit, there is no telling who sent it down, or why. Was the building formerly a restaurant, and this the kitchen? Inside the basement flat, which is real, this sort of realistic speculation can be indulged. But it cannot continue to have meaning once it is applied to the world outside the flat: there can really be no restaurant which would send down orders to a "former" kitchen. Speculation is cut off in mid-breath, is plainly useless.

Yet orders continue to come down and the two men find

themselves under immediate compulsion to fill them, however inadequately. Biscuits, crisps, a bar of chocolate, half a pint of milk—whatever catch-as-catch-can provisions they have brought to the flat with them—are loaded onto the dumb-waiter box and sent up. Still greater demands are returned ("Macaroni Pastitsio. Ormitha Macarounada.") and, in a frenzy of placation, the gunmen part with everything in their packs. In their inadequacy they are humble. Discovering a speaking-tube on the wall, one of them sends a message above "with great deference":

"Good evening. I'm sorry to—bother you, but we just thought we'd better let you know that we haven't got anything left. We sent up all we had. There's no more food down here."

They are not above resenting the sacrifice they have so willingly, so feverishly, made:

"We sent him up all we've got and he's not satisfied. No, honest, it's enough to make the cat laugh. Why did you send him up all that stuff? (*Thoughtfully*) Why did I send it up? (*Pause*) Who knows what he's got upstairs? He's probably got a salad bowl. They must have something up there. They won't get much from down here. You notice they didn't ask for any salads? They've probably got a salad bowl up there. Cold meat, radishes, cucumbers. Watercress. Roll mops."

But the sacrifice was swiftly and unquestioningly made at the time. Only when the moment has passed and the men have begun to exist in a succeeding moment can one of them ask his "thoughtful" question: "Why did I send it up?"

The question is central to the problem of Pinter's curious narrative power. For during all of the time that the gunmen have been desperately trying to meet the demands of the wholly mysterious dumb-waiter, suspense on the stage has grown in proportion to their ignorance of what they were doing. The

[16]

suspense of *The Dumb Waiter* is in very small part due to our awareness that the two men are possibly waiting to kill someone. We are only half-certain that that is their function, their edginess is much more directly concerned with tea-kettles than with potential victims, we cannot fear very greatly for an unspecified victim in any case. The existence of the dumb-waiter is, in addition, apparently irrelevant to the task on which they are engaged; its commands are not necessarily the commands of the unnamed "he" who has hired them, indeed there seems no patterned relationship between the one kind of command and the other. Yet the intrusive, unlooked-for, in a narrative sense distracting activity of the dumb-waiter not only occupies the center of the play but markedly increases its tension.

The command "now" actually agitates the men more than the command "when." When a visitor taps at the door and enters, they are probably going to kill him. About such a matter they can be relatively casual. When a command, any command, is issued in the present tense—even though it has no recognizable source and even though they have no understood obligation—they are terrified.

Mr. Pinter exploits a contemporary form of terror. It would be easy to say that the author's unusual ability to create and maintain suspense in the absence of any defined threat was simply due to his possession of a narrative "gift." That is to say, some writers are born knowing how to tell a story, how to hold an audience—even when the story itself is not inherently fascinating and the audience is not certain that it has been promised any ultimate satisfaction. One kind of novelist, for instance, will write in such a way that the reader is desperately eager to turn the page, though what is on the other side of the page may only lead to the turning of yet another page; the syntax, the entirely personal sense of confiding something urgent, suggests movement. In effect, the pages turn themselves. Another kind of novelist will require conscientious assistance from the reader to keep the book, or the reader's hand, in motion. The pages need lifting, even though they may contain—paragraph by paragraph—arresting details of characterization, valid insights, finely tooled diction.

This is indeed a fact of life: there is such a thing as a narrative "gift." Graham Greene has it; Joyce Cary lacked it. Saul Bellow possesses very little of it, Truman Capote much more. The most ordinary writer of detective fiction probably has it in abundance, or he would not be successful at what he is doing; certainly his other qualities would not guarantee him readers. Yet having or not having a natural narrative power is not a means of distinguishing hacks from their betters, "commercial" writers from serious literary men. In the apocalyptic novels which constitute the literary avant-garde of the moment, the distinction continues to be felt: John Barth's pages turn slowly, Thomas Pynchon's or Gunter Grass's far more rapidly.

And, beyond doubt, Pinter is gifted in this sense: the fact that he has been an actor, and has worked inside the pressure-chamber of stage production, may well have contributed to the development of such felicity at moving forward as he was born with. Yet the particular suspense he achieves is made of something more than a story-teller's lucky ability to make a listener say "And then?" or an actor's instinct for taking center stage and holding it by hook or crook.

A considerable portion of Mr. Pinter's suspense derives from the way that, in pursuing an existentialist method, he sets his plays in motion on a track that runs directly parallel to—or perhaps coincides entirely with—the track on which twentieth-century man feels himself running. It is a track quite different, in its tensions and apprehensions, from any most previous societies have found themselves pressed along.

All societies have found themselves driven by guilt. We find ourselves much more driven by what has been called *angst*, which the dictionary defines as "a feeling of dread, anxiety, or anguish." W. H. Auden has labeled our time "The Age of Anxiety," and the descriptive term has stuck; it was partly out of an effort to explain the prevalence of the sensation that existentialist philosophy came to birth.

There is a simple distinction to be made between the sensation of guilt and that of anxiety. The two are by no means identical. Guilt is felt for a specific crime or sin or failing; apprehension follows because man expects to be punished—in some way—for having permitted himself a particular, well-defined lapse. A man knows what he has done and lives in fear because he has done it.

Anxiety, on the other hand, rises from no single guilty act and fears no clearly spelled-out retribution. It is a general state of mind, a diffused sensation of spiritual and psychological unease which may have its roots in one or twenty of a thousand possible causes but which has no root in any one cause we can name. Anxiety lacks a clear origin. Lacking a clear origin, it lacks a clear ending. We cannot imagine atonement, or any means of freeing ourselves from the sensation, when we cannot say what initiated the sensation, or motivated our fear, to begin with. To use the dictionary again, anxiety—in its psychoanalytical reference—is "the expectancy of evil or danger, without adequate ground." A man who feels guilty always feels guilty about something. But a man in a state of anxiety is anxious about everything—his dread is not confined to responsibility for an act but is distributed throughout his environment and becomes his environment.

Pinter earns his special suspense by constructing his plays in such a way that we are forced to enter this state of mind in the theater. We have not always done so in the theater. When we watch Macbeth grow fearful, even to the point of hallucination, we can make a clear and objective judgment about his fear: he feels as he does because he is guilty of having killed Duncan. We are linking an observed effect to a known cause. We are not undefinably disturbed.

Even during the recent years of our mounting and thoroughly recognized *angst* we have not been accustomed to experiencing in the theater what we have experienced on the streets or at our desks. We may have felt a vague terror at the office, and not known where the animus was coming from. We then went to the theater, observed a man in terror, and saw plainly where his terror came from. The two experiences—one of life, one of art—have not generally coincided. We have felt anxiety on the subway, but seen guilt on the stage. Willy Loman is guilty of having bartered his soul for a smile and a shoeshine. His distress can be diagnosed. Blanche du Bois is to a serious degree guilty of misrepresenting her own nature. Simple exposure to the light will bring her screaming to heel. Such plays look for blame and find it, though the blame may not be confined to a single individual and may indeed attach to an entire social system; wherever it is lodged, the blame can be located. We stand outside the pattern, and know what to expect of it.

Pinter deprives us of our detachment—and our security—by taking us into the pattern. He does so by refusing to say what the pattern is, or by hinting very strongly that there is no pattern. Bewildered, we look about us for points of reference. Finding none, we begin to share the anxiety of the characters whose lives we can observe but cannot chart. We no longer judge their collective state of mind. We inhabit it.

The act of unpatterning is therefore of great importance in the working out of any Pinter scenario. Whatever action is taking place must have no clear beginning, which is to say it must not have originated in a guilty act. In this way the past is eliminated as a conscious source of worry and the two men of *The Dumb Waiter* are bound to the tense "now" of commands which are without cause or precedent. The two men become tense on the instant because the position in which they find themselves is, to them as to us, unintelligible. Instead of passing from past crime to future punishment, they stand trembling before all possibility.

Similarly, whatever action is taking place must have no foreseeable future, which is to say that there are no logical, deducible consequences coming from an earlier crime or event. The earlier crime or event has not been specified, and therefore cannot have preordained consequences. Thus the future is also eliminated, as we have seen, as a reasonable source of worry. There are no reasons why Rose should be dispossessed of her room—she has done nothing to deserve uprooting—or why she should expect a visitor from downstairs. A reasonable worry is, in a way, a comfort. It is only the altogether unreasonable, perched on the shoulder of the "now," that is altogether terrifying.

With the past gone from the pattern because no prior guilty act can be attributed to anyone, and with the future gone from the pattern because no deserved and identified threat looms ahead, the pattern itself disintegrates into a shapeless immediacy, a fearful moving-about among objects and persons that are directly present but are without histories or discoverable essences. All persons, all objects are now to be feared—and revered, in the sense that they produce awe—because no one of them can be isolated as a single source of apprehension. A major part of Pinter's suspense, then, derives from his drawing us into the unpatterned *angst* which we know well enough in the dusty uncertainty of our days but which we normally keep at arm's length in the playhouse by insisting that the playwright show

[21]

us cause and effect, crime and punishment. "Step into my parlor," Mr. Pinter says. We do so, feeling like so many flies, wondering where the spider is.

Perhaps it is easy enough to understand why we should feel effectively dislocated in rooms which may or may not have floors above or below them, or why we should feel a nameless anxiety in the face of commands being issued from wholly invisible sources in a restaurant above. These things are rumors, and rumors are always unsettling precisely because their origins cannot be traced or their effects anticipated.

But how is this faceless menace to be sustained as an effect in the theater when it acquires an actual face, when it is clearly and physically embodied in a character who walks in at the door to confront another, quickly quailing, character? If the threat is no longer a matter of hearsay, or of mysteriously delivered messages from nowhere, but an actual, breathing, talking, even obviously violent human being, hasn't the threat now been made concrete, tangible, defined on the spot? And aren't we back to regulation playmaking in which protagonist and antagonist face one another in broad daylight to thrash matters out?

In Pinter's first full-length play, *The Birthday Party*, also written in 1957, perfectly tangible confrontations of this sort are arranged. In outline, the play would seem to contain all of the standard paraphernalia of old-fashioned stage melodrama, or of the suspense film. We are concerned with a victim who is being hemmed in by apparent gangsters who mean to "take him for a ride," and the hemming-in is done openly on the stage. How shall this sort of danger remain nameless and faceless? And why?

We first meet Stanley, a man in his late thirties, some sort of concert pianist whose career has deteriorated, who now spends his time in a seaside boarding-house, sleeping late. He could probably still play piano on the local pier if he wanted to. If he doesn't want to, it is because he feels the effort would be futile. He has been systematically persecuted, driven from his profession. The last time he attempted a concert he found the hall closed, firmly shuttered up against him without so much as a caretaker about. He remembers the occasion as he would a nightmare. "They'd locked it up," he says, wiping his spectacles on his pyjama jacket, "A fast one. They pulled a fast one. . . . They want me to crawl down on my bended knees."

We next meet his enemies. "They" are no longer invisible hands sending peremptory messages by a dumb-waiter. "They" appear most tangibly in the persons of Goldberg and McCann, strangers carrying suitcases who wish to take rooms in the same boarding-house. Stanley tries to drive them away. They cannot be budged. Stanley defends himself before them. They cannot be won over. Ultimately, under their prodding and baiting and because of the sheer fact of their presence, Stanley suffers something like a nervous breakdown, becomes violent. Now Stanley is led off by Goldberg and McCann. The last thing we hear is "the sound of a car going away."

The confrontation is so direct and sustained that it is almost as though Rose had met her man from the basement early in the play, or as though the thugs of *The Dumb Waiter* were face to face, from the beginning, with the man they were hired to kill. We seem close to a play in which fear is reasonably motivated and in which the parties to the struggle are clearly identified. We are dealing with beginnings and ends, with patterns, again.

But are we? As it happens, no one in the play understands the pattern through which he is moving. Presumably, Stanley is being repaid for something he has done in the past, for some betrayal or other. But Stanley cannot quite remember his past, not even his father's address. Of one thing he feels certain: he's not the "sort of bloke to—cause any trouble." In the last place he lived, the place in which he might be thought to have done whatever it is Goldberg and McCann think he has done, he "never stepped outside the door."

Goldberg and McCann, though they seem to have a clear duty to carry out now, are no clearer about the impulses that have propelled them into motion. They are not personal enemies of Stanley, though they personally—and very viciously—rough him up. There is vague talk of an "organization" which Stanley has betrayed, but Goldberg and McCann give no indication of being insiders to that organization. They are emissaries, set on a certain course by an irresistible force outside them, but they are not intimates of the force at work nor are they even capable of thinking about it coherently. When Goldberg attempts to state his beliefs about the world and its patterning his mind stammers to a halt, becoming first "vacant," then "desperate," then "lost."

This is a blind collision. Existentially, it reports an experience we have not yet dealt with. Though each man exists uniquely in the void, straining to discover his identity and unable to relate intelligibly to other creatures like him, he is not sole inhabitant of the void. The void is like the vault of heaven in which shooting stars may, without warning and for no immediately discernible reason, cross paths and even crash into one another. Each shooting star follows its own orbit. It cannot help doing so. It is following the laws of the "organization." But two separate courses, initiated by two separate impulses, may come into conjunction at any time, and most tangibly. Two isolated forces enter an area simultaneously, behaving simply as they behave.

The principals in this central struggle—Stanley, Goldberg, McCann—exist. Because they exist, they act. They do not act out of prior definition; they are on the way to discovering themselves but they have not yet done so. Their gestures are not dictated by conscious roles, by a shared nature, by given melodramatic or metaphysical postulates. They are alive and free to do whatever they will do, but their activity is a probing process, not a disclosing one. They are finding out what they are by what they do and by what is done to them. There is no master-plan; there is only an experimental testing.

Any man who is in the process of achieving his identity is bound to meet, bump into, recoil from, affect, and be affected by other men engaged in the same process that occupies him. It is a historical accident that any two such orbits should coincide, since the overlapping paths are separately initiated and not logically related. But the overlapping, the collision, has consequences.

One man sets one foot into space, to see what it does. Another does the same thing at the same time. The two meet, and the meeting may be disastrous for one or the other or both. One thrust foot may prove stronger than another thrust foot. Each foot will contend for the space with the equipment it actually has, will struggle for what seems power but is actually definition. The encounter will end in some way or other. But it has not been a planned encounter, and it will not have an effect-from-cause ending. Only the encounter is recorded, in its suddenness, in its blindness, in its mystery. Yes, the encounter has a result. But the result is a fact, not an explanation or an interpretation. Pinter does not invite interpretation. "Sound of a car driving away."

This blind encounter is dramatized in a simpler and more literal way in a later full-length play, *The Caretaker*, written in 1959. Here a homeless, shiftless, scrofulous, exceedingly self-righteous old man encounters a younger man who voluntarily offers him living-space in his quarters. The generous act is not

[25]

logically motivated; the old man cannot grasp why he has been taken in—though he is quick to come in, and quick to demand more than he has been offered—nor can he in any other way fathom the mind of his benefactor. His benefactor's mind is in fact unfathomable: he has earlier been subjected to a frontal lobotomy.

The old man next encounters his host's brother. This brother is sly, taunting, hostile—though again for no cause the old man can discover. The two encounters coincide in time but are not organically linked in the sense that they can explain each other; they are wholly baffling to the mind enduring them, and they are actual. The old man is given an actual pair of shoes, an actual bag is handed to him by one brother and snatched away by the other. The play confines us to the sensations of the man to whom these things happen, and for just so long as they are happening. At the end of the play they cease happening. The old man continues talking, but he is talking now to silence. He has had the experience of colliding with two other forces which exist precisely as he does: as self-determining isolates whose "natures" have not yet been resolved. There has been a meeting, a bumping, an abrasion. The meeting has been suspenseful because anything at all could happen. The three men in the room do not come from a common matrix which might enable them to predict one another. They go on finding themselves through what they cannot find in others.

Pinter maintains his mystery, even when his menacing forces are perfectly visible and in head-on confrontation, by carefully denying them psychological access to one another. They are face to face and still impenetrable. They have not yet acquired essences that can be detected.

Though there is a degree of violence, or of sensed menace, in every Pinter play, the plays are not straightforward melodramas. Comedy is the constant companion of threat, and some-times the threat itself contains an elusive comic edge. The messages from the dumb-waiter make the gunmen who are re-ceiving them apprehensive; they also make us laugh, sometimes openly, sometimes nervously.

Apart from the fact that the playwright himself has a knack for the curtly phrased retort that, read blandly, has an air of amusing insult about it—he has, in fact, written a group of revue sketches—the very methods he employs, and the shifting-sands vision of man's precarious existence which these methods re-cord, tend naturally toward one kind of comedy.

Comedy has always made capital of mistaken identity. When one man is taken for another, or one thing taken for another, we are invariably surprised and most often delighted that such easy interchanges should prove to be so possible, that the uni-verse should turn out to be so slippery. *The Comedy of Errors* is a root comic design: one looks into a face and cannot say whose face it is.

Existentialist uncertainty is, of course, not so blithe in tone as a mere tumbling about of twins. Not being able to tell one twin from another has a clear logic inside it to guide and com-fort us: we know the "natural" cause of our confusion and can readily respond to it without any admixture of dismay. The Pinter approach is necessarily darker than this, for we look into a face and find ourselves unable to name it without being able to explain, on the spot, our bafflement. The effect is more closely related to another standard comic device: the business, say, of passing a graveyard at night, seeing an object moving among the tombstones and prickling in terror—only to have it turn out to be a cat. In *The Caretaker*, and in the dark, a buzz-ing, bright-eyed monster seems to move with seething teeth across a room: it turns out to be a vacuum-cleaner.

Mistakes of this sort always strike us as funny not only

[27]

because, in the aftermath, we are relieved to find them un-menacing; fundamentally we are amused that, in a tangible world made up of sharply defined shapes and perfectly hard surfaces, any two unlikes should be able to blend into such a momentary like. A sensation of giddiness overwhelms us: what has frightened us shouldn't have, it is absurd that we should have responded so disproportionately; we have participated in an incongruity.

The fright is not forgotten, nor should it be: it is perfectly possible to be killed by a vacuum-cleaner or, for that matter, to be clawed by a cat. We never can know when vacuum-cleaner or cat is going to turn on us. We might well be disturbed, in addition, by our awareness that we can make such mistakes. Our equipment for detecting reality is not all that it might be. Yet there is no getting away from the laughter that follows and was inherent in the situation all the time: we have used our eyes and been made fools of.

Following *The Caretaker*, Mr. Pinter turned his attention, in two shorter plays originally written for television, to what is lightly amusing in the ambiguity imbedded in his premises. *The Collection* (1961) and *The Lover* (1965) are both a great deal more than revue sketches: but here the scales are tipped to favor what is funny in our inability to define one another, or ourselves.

The Collection takes place in two simultaneously visible flats. One is shared by Harry and Bill, both dress-designers; though there are no explicit homosexual gestures, Harry is jealous of Bill. The other flat houses James and Stella, husband and wife, operators of a boutique. There has been a fashion display in Leeds the week before; both Stella, from the one flat, and Bill, from the other, have gone to it. Stella and Bill may have met in a hotel corridor, just outside an elevator, kissed on impulse, and spent the night together. Stella's husband thinks she has slept with Bill and he calls, unannounced, on Bill to get at the truth. Harry is equally concerned that Bill has slept with Stella; he calls upon Stella to urge her to break off the relationship.

But there is nothing to say—for certain—that there has been any relationship. Stella may be lying (boasting? teasing? tormenting?) when she seems to admit the affair to her husband. Bill, pressed to confess by James, may confess simply because he is expected to or because it amuses him to do so. All parties are sparring. No party knows the other well enough to say what he might or might not do. Around musical chairs the four contestants go; in a fashion reminiscent of Pirandello, each makes the other into the image he has of him.

There is no violent pressure here, simply an anxious—though generally polite—need to define. All are poised, self-controlled, in cool command of a situation that is endlessly open. James, intruding upon Bill, behaves as though he were in his own flat, not Bill's; he asks Bill what he would like to drink. Bill, at first dismissing the night in Leeds as a bit of pure fantasy Stella has invented ("Really rather naughty of her") pauses to ask her husband "Do you know her well?"

If neither of them can know Stella absolutely—is she a whore or is she putting it all on?—neither can they quite know themselves. James and Bill spend a moment, side by side, looking into a mirror, though James expects nothing to come of mirrors: "They're deceptive."

A degree of violence does obtrude before this psychological parlor game has run its course. Bill, backing away from James, tumbles over a piece of furniture and suddenly finds himself wondering whether James will permit him to rise again or whether he is about to lash out at him with his feet. During a subsequent meeting, James and Bill contemplate a duel with fruitknives, and there is in fact some minor bloodshed. But the comic emphasis is maintained even at knife's-edge. Bill, ready

[29]

to shrug the contest off, announces that he is putting his knife down.

JAMES. Well, I'll pick it up.

James does so and faces him with two knives.

BILL. Now you've got two.

JAMES. I've got another one in my hip pocket.

Pause.

BILL. What do you do, swallow them?

Ignorance has a preposterous side to it, and it is possible to be flippant about it. In the end, the play refuses to perspire over the problem of identity. James returns home to Stella, who is playing with her kitten. He has decided for himself, or rather he wishes to decide for himself, that Stella and Bill didn't really "do anything" in Leeds. If they met, they merely sat in the hotel lounge and chatted. If they discussed going to Stella's room, the discussion was hypothetical, the projected act unrealized.

JAMES. . . . That's the truth, isn't it?

Pause.

You just sat and talked about what you would do, if you went to your room. That's what you did.

Pause.

Didn't you?

Pause.

That's the truth . . . isn't it?

End of play, with Stella looking at James, "neither confirming nor denying," her face "friendly and sympathetic." Uncertainty may be a tolerable condition of life if one has the patient good sense to cock an eye at it whimsically.

The Lover is even lighter, very close to extended vaudeville, though, in its existential playfulness, it opens the door to yet another aspect of the continuing proposition that existence precedes essence.

"Is your lover coming today?" Richard asks his wife, Sarah, as the curtain rises. Richard is leaving for his office, where he is pictured as slaving over ledgers all day, but he is concerned with Sarah's happiness and he wishes to be sure that she'll have a "pleasant afternoon." Returning in the evening, he solicitously inquires how the afternoon went. Sarah, equally considerate, supposes that Richard has a mistress. This, as it turns out, is not quite the case.

RICHARD. But I haven't got a mistress. I'm very well acquainted with a whore, but I haven't got a mistress. There's a world of difference.

SARAH. A whore?

RICHARD. (*Taking an olive*) Yes. Just a common or garden slut. Not worth talking about. Handy between trains, nothing more.

Though Richard and Sarah pride themselves on "frankness at all costs" because frankness is "essential to a healthy marriage," Sarah confesses that she is surprised by the news that Richard has a whore. "Why?" Richard asks. "I wasn't looking for your double, was I?"

At this point—it is one of the few instances in which Pinter's surprises are not so surprising—we begin to leap ahead of the playwright. Yes, the lover who comes to visit Sarah in the afternoons is Richard. And Sarah is Richard's whore, her own double and not her double. Such a visit is dramatized and the two behave entirely differently to each other. Indeed, when Richard the lover speculates on whether or not he'd hit it off with Richard the husband, supposing their paths ever crossed, Sarah thinks not. "You've got very little in common," she points out.

What makes this relatively brief conceit more interesting than a simple, and fairly obvious, vaudeville "switch" is its introduction of the notion that both Richard and Sarah truly possess the two separate identities they assume. They are not children playing bawdy-house. They are adults who are other adults than themselves, unconfined by one or another social role. Looked at conventionally, *The Lover* might simply seem to be saying that married couples need to pretend a bit now and then in order to refresh their relationship. Or, conceivably, it might seem to be saying that in a highly structured society sexual impulses are rarely given free play and that some subterfuge is needed to release such impulses even in marriage. Looked at existentially, it says another thing altogether: no woman is essentially wife or essentially whore, she is potentially either or both at once; the same duality, or multiplicity, holds true for the husband-lover. Personality is not something given; it is fluid.

In the earlier *The Collection* no character could say what another was; but there was always the lingering assumption that, if only one could see clearly enough or probe persistently enough, a firm, fixed identity—a "truth"—might be uncovered. Here, in *The Lover*, we do see clearly enough, we walk directly into the situation as though we had walked into that hotel room in Leeds. And what we see, now that we see clearly, is that nothing human is fixed, everything human is mobile. The same woman can be a whore in a hotel room and an innocent playing with her kitten at home while remaining the same woman, without contradiction.

If existence precedes essence, and if plays are to be written in such a way as to reveal this sequence, then no character on a stage dares be essentially anything: husband, wife, lover, whore, brother, father, beggar, host. Instead, character is potency, possibility, movement.

We are touching now on that freedom of movement, without prior direction or definition, to which Sartre says man is "condemned" and which constitutes man's exploration of the void in search of his realized, until now unknown, self. Categories and traditional roles contain no man, unless he lets himself be contained by them, choosing to conform to a pattern that does not actually express his potency. Man cannot be described except in terms of motion: he is what he does next. And there may be another "next" after that, which means that there will then be a new, and still unfinished, "is."

In two thematically related plays, *A Slight Ache* (1961) and *The Homecoming* (1965), Pinter has gone on to examine identity as movement, not as category. In *The Homecoming* the issue is made most explicit, set forth in a single speech. The men about Ruth are debating categories. A table is a table, just as a wife is a wife.

RUTH. Don't be too sure though. You've forgotten something. Look at me. I . . . move my leg. That's all it is. But I wear . . . underwear . . . which moves with me . . . it . . . captures your attention. Perhaps you misinterpret. The action is simple. It's a leg . . . . moving. My lips move. Why don't you restrict . . . your observations to that? Perhaps the fact that they move is more significant . . . than the words which come through them. You must bear that . . . possibility . . . in mind.

The possibility is going to have consequences a few scenes later. But it may be best to glance at *A Slight Ache* first, not so much because it was written earlier, but because in it the contrast between category and movement is more simply and swiftly outlined.

A man—and for Pinter the male now tends to become the categorist—is baffled by the presence of an old, filthy matchseller who stands at the bottom of the lane near his house daily. There are very few passersby. The old man never sells any matches. Why does he come? The householder cannot let the question alone; he becomes feverish in his anxiety to know the answer. He invites the ragged presence into the house, offers him a drink, cajoles him, coaxes him, finally commands him to say who he is and what he is doing. The match-seller never utters a word. His inquisitor is now half-mad with frustration, distressed by his inability to define.

The householder's wife enters, and takes over. She asks no questions. She simply embraces the visitor. She is, that is to say, open to him and to his possibility. Shortly, she installs him in the house. The husband goes out to sell matches.

The woman here is readily seen as catalyst, as the agent of change. And she is. Through her the husband drops his "role" as husband and as categorist and finds himself assuming another role he could not have anticipated, cannot even now define. Through her the match-seller, still silent, becomes partner. But she is not merely an agent of action in the play, mistress of shifting possibilities. She is herself in motion, and it is her own assumption of a second identity—wife-mother to the match-seller—that is the central gesture of the play. She has been one thing; without hesitation, she moves forward to become another. Questions of identity—her own, or anyone else's—do not concern her, as they have so concerned her husband. She is what she finds it within herself to be, she is the movement she finds herself making.

The situation, with its altering relationships, is repeated in the climactic sequence of *The Homecoming*. Ruth is Teddy's wife and has come, after some years of marriage, to visit her husband's family. Teddy, her husband, is the categorist par excellence. He is a Doctor of Philosophy at an American university. For him, everything is fixed. He has seen stability. "To see, to be able to *see!*" he exclaims. "I'm the one who can see. That's why I can write my critical works." He is proud of his "intellectual equilibrium" and a shade contemptuous of those who move uncertainly about him. "You're just objects. You just

. . . move about. I can observe it. I can see what you do. . . . But you're lost in it. . . . I won't be lost in it."

Teddy is rigid and detached, wedded to essences, a Platonist. Once more there are intruders with whom he cannot be comfortable: his father and two brothers. The father and two brothers, observing Ruth and her presence as motion, make Ruth a proposition. Let Teddy go back to America, let her remain with them as their "whore." They will give her a flat and furnishings, they will enable her to pay for these by leasing her out some nights to other men, they will take turns being with her and being whatever they can be to her. She will be whatever she can be to them. Ruth, having embraced one brother in a dance and the other in a copulative roll-about on the couch, accepts the proposition.

Teddy accepts Ruth's acceptance of the proposition. He is not so anxious about identities as the husband of *A Slight Ache;* he is certain that he has arrived at them, he is beyond becoming involved; he does, however, go into exile as surely as his predecessor does. As he leaves, there is no sign of animus, rejection, or even finality in Ruth. "Don't become a stranger" is the last thing she says to him.

The woman, Ruth, is the center of the play because she is the existential suppleness of the play. She continues to become her identity. She has been wife, mother, daughter-in-law, sister-in-law. But these roles are not terminal, they are not permitted to become absolutes. "Whore" is a part of her possibility, too. Neither is "whore" to be regarded as terminal, as defining. Who is to say what movement lies beyond, before the self comes to be the self? When does the movement of lips, legs, underwear cease, saying, in sum, "This is I"?

Pinter uses the "whore" image repeatedly—it has appeared in three out of the last four plays we have discussed—precisely because the whore, by definition, lacks definition. The whore performs no single social role, she is what each new man wishes to make of her. She is available to experience, and she is an available experience. She is eternally "between trains," she is known in passing and as something passing. In fact, she is simply unknown. Existentially speaking, we are all life's whores to the degree that we are in motion and have not arbitrarily codified and thereby stilled ourselves.

Rich man, poor man, beggar man, thief—the picaresque hero, who is generally something of a whore, is all of these in turn, which is no doubt why the picaresque hero has enjoyed a considerable revival under existentialist pressure. Viewed in an existentialist light, each of us is picaresque-hero-whore: permanently subject to unpredictable intrusion, to the unlooked-for event and the unthinkable proposition. Until we have actually responded to these things—actually moved and behaved in the circumstances they create—we cannot say what our response, or our very selves, might be. It is only when responsive movement has been exhausted that we can lay claim to knowing essence.

In the contemporary theater Pinter's work is original in method and unique in its effect upon the stage. An Arnold Wesker and a John Arden can be related in intention and style. Beckett and Ionesco have sunspots in common. It is possible to put John Osborne and Edward Albee side by side and see that they raise their disturbances with much the same lift of voice. But Pinter's territory is very private territory. He has drawn upon a philosophical disposition that is very much in the air and available to everyone, true. But he is the one man who has fought essence to a standstill, refused it houseroom until he has finished moving freely about.

"I don't know what kind of characters my plays will have until they . . . well, until they *are*," he has said. "Until they indicate to me what they are. . . . Once I've got the clues, I follow them—that's my job, really, to follow clues. . . . I follow what I see on the paper in front of me—one sentence after another. That doesn't mean I don't have a dim, possible overall idea—the image that starts off doesn't just engender what happens immediately, it engenders the possibility of an overall happening, which carries me through. I've got an idea of what *might* happen—sometimes I'm absolutely right, but on many occasions I've been proved wrong by what does actually happen."

The play is discovery in the way that personality, under existentialism, is discovery. It has not been fashioned to fit a hard and fast idea about man, or society, or the nature of things. "I distrust ideological statements of any kind," the playwright adds.

He has been remarkably successful in constructing a series of felt realities that do not depend upon conceptual underpinning: the experience of entirely tangible places unmoored in a void, the experience of living and fearing and even laughing in the present tense without knowledge of past or future, the experience of encountering other objects just as impenetrable as we are as we jockey for position in a swarming, footloose universe, the experience of never being certain what gesture any man may make next because everyman is, at the present writing, incomplete.

These are not statements made in the plays. They are the movement of the plays. The play is only an event, not a logical demonstration; the event must speak, illogically but persuasively, for itself. The play persuades by existing, and in no other way. If it failed to persuade in this way, no theory—however correct, however contemporary—could save it. Pinter takes his uncertainty seriously.

Perfectly? Of course not. Playwrights have a habit of not

being perfect, and in this case a writer is attempting a break not only with recently conventional modes of playmaking but with a kind of thinking that has simply been reflexive with us since Plato. It's not surprising that he doesn't entirely escape conceptualization, try as he may.

Clearly there is something schematic and preformed in his recurring use of the male as conceptualist, the female as existentialist, the male as rigid, the female as flexible. Such an observation may, of course, be true enough; it is even a very old one, echoing the ancient contrast between the male as rational, the female as intuitive. But it does suggest a return to a belief in essential natures—the mind of the universe has made man this way, women that way—which tends to contradict the author's own insistence that the moving lip is more important than the word it forms. There is also a shade of inadvertent irony here: Mr. Pinter, a male, is categorizing his own kind as somewhat incapable of the open and free action which he, the male playwright, is committed to exploring. No doubt he detects his inherited tendency to conceptualize when he doesn't want to.

The schematic pursues him in other ways. The frontal lobotomy which has been performed upon the benevolent brother in *The Caretaker*, for instance, very literally freezes that character into an essential position. This man is fixed, his patterns are determined, he cannot be further altered by any free forward movement of his own. The use of the lobotomy is, I think, a vulgarization in Pinter's terms: it is too easy, too expedient a way of saying that communication has been cut off. Instead of the mysteriously impenetrable we have here the symbolically impenetrable; the figure becomes a concept, as in Beckett, rather than an unpredictable, fluid force.

Actually, *The Caretaker* is a kind of battleground of styles, an unresolved tug-of-war between older methods of characterization and the newer method Pinter is reaching for. The play really functions in three degrees of perspective: we look at it as we might a toy theater in which three cut-out figures had been placed in different slots in the floor, at different distances from us. The caretaker himself, the garrulous and tenacious old man, is nearest to us, full-bodied in a familiar way, as rounded-out and complete as an ebullient whiner out of Dickens. We know him utterly. There is nothing unfinished or elusive about him. He is perfectly realized. But he is realized, in his wrapped-up complexity, in what here must be called an old-fashioned way.

The benevolent brother occupies the middle distance. He is symbolic man, two-dimensional, forever representing the same value, as he might in Beckett or certainly would in *Everyman*. He stands for an impasse, and has no other qualities, unless he can be said to have the quality of hinting that only the mentally destroyed are given to kindness in a violent universe intent upon exercising power to determine identity. He is a morality-play figure.

The inexplicably hostile brother, threatening even in his sporadic geniality, is placed in the far distance, nearest the shadows. He is the man Pinter's hand is most often after, all change and motion and indeterminateness, perpetual mocker of proposed stabilities. The others in the play have plans. So does he, in a whimsical and obviously untrustworthy way. But all plans dissolve as he touches them. His very presence destroys plan, exposes it for the mirage it is. He is the unfinished, the unascertainable, the existentialist man.

We are apt to like the caretaker most, simply because we are accustomed, in our theatergoing, to his sort of complex but firmly defined being. But the hostile brother, the taunting one who refuses us access to himself because the self is not ready to be named, is the presence in the play that leads us most directly into the Pinter landscape as a whole. He is, indeed, the only figure in the play to do the new thing most persistently and characteristically pursued by the playwright: behave before he has been pigeon-holed. Strictly speaking, the three men probably do not belong in the same play: each comes from a separate and somewhat isolated literary world; none can really move from one slot, one dimension, to another. This difficulty does keep the lines of communication down, which is an existentialist requirement. But it achieves that particular effect by a mixing of modes, and at some cost to stylistic unity.

Curiously, explicit violence is also a troubling, and not quite assimilated, element in the playwright's work. So long as violence is threatened, intimated, promised, the chill in the air is actual and the atmosphere of the play uncorrupted. But whenever the sinuous, seeking movement of the play breaks open into concrete deed, into physical definiteness, an aura of the stage-trick, the artificial climax, the merely surprising act-curtain intrudes. The sudden death at the end of *The Dumb Waiter* is surprising, and in that sense theatrically effective; but it also leaves us with a feeling of having been taken in by mere Grand Guignol. The entrance of the Negro, the savage assault upon him, and the instant blindness of Rose at the end of *The Room* have a similar flavor of the startling for its own sake, or for the sake of getting the curtain down on a sufficiently defiant and baffling note. In *The Birthday Party* there is some feeling that we are losing the play as Stanley loses his self-control in the deliberately explosive nightmare of his attack upon Lulu.

Why is the deed sometimes less persuasive than the rumor of deeds to come? I suspect precisely because it is a defined act, which means that it terminates the groping forward that is the whole environment in an existentialist view of things. To kill someone is to put a name, a meaning, an identity upon the situation before us. The condition that is being dramatized has come to an end. But the end must be arbitrary because no

[40]

existentialist is yet ready to say that he knows ends, that he can announce essences.

Pinter confesses that he likes "a good curtain," and some of his eruptions may simply come from a craftsman's passion for good stage-rigging. The stylistic problem remains unresolved, however. If existence is endlessly open, where is it to be closed? If movement is all, who dares stop it?

One last qualification. I find myself preferring the shorter plays—plays which may run anywhere from thirty minutes to an hour and a half—to the full-length extensions of Pinter's highly individual vision. *A Slight Ache*, for instance, seems to me to do the work of *The Homecoming*, or a very great deal of it, with a succinctness and a sustained tension that are distributed and seriously dissipated in the longer play.

In its last half hour, *The Homecoming* is going to feel its way to the same sort of unstable equation that keeps *A Slight Ache* poised on the edge of dissolving identities for as long as it lasts. But while *The Homecoming* is postponing its eventual plunge into movement, it has little to do but execute a delaying ballet of intimation, of carefully crossed legs and carefully concealed potentiality.

Marking time during the delay, Pinter tends to fill in with the near-exhausted devices of the conceptual Theater of the Absurd. In particular, he doesn't mind borrowing from Ionesco, spacing out his contradictions mathematically. Max, the father of the family, expands on the theme of his wife, who had "a heart of gold," and his "three fine grown-up lads." A minute later these same folk are "three bastard sons" and "a slutbitch of a wife." The device is more deeply imbedded in tangible character than it ever is in Ionesco, where two sides of a face pull apart as though they had been pasted together out of cut paper. It is also relevant to the infinite-identity theme. Nonetheless, it is an echo, too conceptually planned, transparently technical, wholly verbal. It is not life itself in unreined flux, as we shall find life behaving toward the end of the play.

Why should the longer plays delay, or circle, a situation that can be accounted for quite satisfactorily in a tight forty minutes? I suspect that it has not quite occurred to Mr. Pinter that it is possible to display more than a single altering step into the void, a single transposition of personality, a single throw of the existentialist dice, in any one play. There is nothing, really, to prevent him from moving forward again once the initial elision has taken place. Having moved from wife–mother to whore, Ruth may very well move to yet another extension of being. Since she is not predefined, she is free to go on taking steps without worrying about the kind of footprints she leaves or what prying detectives may make of them. One gesture is not definition, is not the end of things. A play might very well take us through three or four persons in one, as *Hamlet* does, before it chooses to curtail its possibly endless investigation of possibility. There is nothing in the method to say that we must stop at Stage Two. Thus far Mr. Pinter tends to confine himself to a first change of state, a practice which makes many of the shorter plays perfect but which attenuates, and makes repetitive, the longer ones.

I have mentioned *Hamlet*, which calls for a further remark. Mr. Pinter has described himself, and not necessarily baitingly, as "a traditional playwright." The fact of the matter is that there is a theatrical tradition of pursuing existence without being certain of essence—it came into being long before any philosopher elected to challenge Plato in so many words—and it has given us some of our most cherished, if hotly debated, masterpieces. It would seem very likely that Shakespeare traced Hamlet's course without any dead-certain concept in his head of where Hamlet's quest was to end. Death, yes, most

[42]

likely, though in Shakespeare's source-legend Hamlet doesn't die. But precisely how the tangle of personality was to unravel itself, when and where it was to assert itself as defined, seems bafflingly open throughout Shakespeare's play. Now cruel, now kind, now dedicated, now dilatory, now—but we have gone over these unpredictable alterations in Hamlet forever. It is the very lack of a sensed master-plan, or a conceptual program for the play, that has led to the sort of exasperation with *Hamlet* for lacking "an objective correlative" that T. S. Eliot felt. In the end, Mr. Eliot controlled his exasperation and took his criticism back. Why? Because, "objective correlative" or no, Hamlet existed. Critics may quarrel about Hamlet's essential nature to the end of time. But Hamlet stirred first, and still stirs.

Thus, in a sense, Pinter is returning us to a "tradition" at the same time that he insists upon destroying what we call tradition. The stage has always been open, in spite of the rigors philosophers have imposed upon thought, to the tasting of experience experimentally. Its very nature tempts it to do so. The stage is an arena, a bear-bit, a bull-ring, an empty space until challengers enter it. Who is to say what all challengers are to do on the spur of the moment, in the heat of passion, under the pressure of the contest? Bear-pits and bull-rings breed surprises. Claw and cape behave differently on different days, in different winds. An arena is an open, initially empty, space not because it is a place for fighting but because it is a place for finding, for discovery, for realization. It first gapes at us as though it were a great question mark. Then movement fills it and—perhaps—makes a shape.

We tend to forget that this is a possible theatrical tradition or a possible playwriting method because we have lately lived so long under another dispensation: that of the "well-made play," the play built of bricks selected to shore up a thesis, the play dominated by a writer's logic. This later, neater, more predictable method has wearied us for a considerable time. We have understood its virtues, its enclosed intellectual systems and its clear time-and-thought sequences well enough; but we have intuited, all along, that drama had something less reasonable and more impulsive to say to us, given its other voice.

Pinter might be called "traditional" in the sense that he has begun to restore, under the fresh questioning of a twentieth-century philosophical method, an old and neglected urge to enter the arena naked, without the support of tried-and-true tricks or proved propositions but with a firm determination to move as much as a man may move against whatever can be made to yield to him. When Euripides entered such an arena in *The Bacchae* it was probably without hope of fully resolving the contest between Dionysiac excess and Dionysiac rectitude. But in he went, all the way, giving every god and devil his due, to see what an uninhibited probing, an unrestricted invasion of the Greeks' very own void, might uncover. Conceptualization, prior commitment, would surely have stopped him short of the play's boundless frontier, its resolute pressing forward into the infinite. Asking only how extensively any one force might assert itself, he made—out of such a reaching—an ambiguous, deeply mystifying, blood-curdling masterpiece. He did not seek to devise or support a system, as Aeschylus had done in *The Eumenides*. Focusing his eyes beyond system, he sought instead to see all that was.

At the same time, Pinter is obviously untraditional in that he has almost fully freed himself from the realistic–naturalistic "problem-play" notion that drama is best constructed as a syllogism, with a conclusion following inevitably from known postulates. He is also untraditional in that he has accepted, for the lip moves first and that its "nature" as lip comes later—practical dramatic purposes, the post-Greek proposition that

BIOGRAPHICAL AND BIBLIOGRAPHICAL NOTE

Harold Pinter was born on October 10, 1930, the son of a Jewish tailor, in Hackney, East London, a point at which the metropolis trails off into the seedier countryside. He attended Hackney Downs Grammar School, where he played Macbeth, apparently well. He went on to train himself for the stage at the Royal Academy of Dramatic Arts and the Central School of Speech and Drama, then acted under the name of David Baron with various repertory companies between 1949 and 1957, among them the Anew McMaster group which played one-night stands across Ireland. Between engagements, he worked as a waiter, a doorman, a dish-washer, and a door-to-door book salesman; he began an autobiographical novel which later became the partial basis for his play *The Dwarfs;* he was excused from military service as a conscientious objector; and in 1956 he married the actress Vivien Merchant, whom he had met while touring.

In 1957, when he was twenty-six, he turned to playwriting; the first productions of his plays were done in school theaters (the Bristol University Drama Department, the Bristol Old Vic Drama School) and in the "private club" playhouses which constitute a kind of specially licensed British off-Broadway (The Hampstead Theater Club, The Royal Court Theater, the Arts Theater Club). A production of *The Birthday Party*, under Mr. Pinter's direction, was presented at both Oxford and Cambridge before venturing to London; in London it was received with such indifference that the first Thursday matinee played to exactly six people. *The Caretaker* became Mr. Pinter's first commercial success, with a record run at the Duchess Theater and an award from *The Evening Standard* as the best play of 1960.

Since that time Mr. Pinter has also worked in films, radio, and television. For films he has written *The Servant, The Pumpkin Eater, The Compartment, The Quiller Memorandum*, and *Accident*. Several of his theatrical successes were first radio and television plays, and in 1965 *The Tea-Party* was commissioned for performance, under the auspices of the BBC and the European Broadcasting Union, in sixteen European countries. Mr. Pinter was created CBE in the 1966 Birthday Honours.

[46]

after the utterance and because of it. He does not particularly care whether "nature" or "essence" is absolutely arrived at within the confines of his activity as continuing observer. As a dramatist, he wishes to observe in the same way that, as man and householder, he wishes to live.

"I'm bored by what New York thinks of itself," he has said on one of his visits to the United States. "I wish it would shut up." Even cities are better off not trying to define themselves too precisely too soon. "There's a little village in Gloucestershire, in the Cotswold Hills, that I like better. The village is called Bibury. It's very English. It just exists."

Esslin, Martin. The Theatre of the Absurd. New York, Anchor, 1961.

—— "Harold Pinter, un dramaturge anglais de l'absurde." *Preuves*, No. 151 (1964) 45–54.

—— "Godot and His Children: the Theatre of Samuel Beckett and Harold Pinter." *Experimental Drama*, XIV (1965) 128–46.

Leech, Clifford. "Two Romantics, Arnold Wesker and Harold Pinter." *Contemporary Theatre*, XX (1964) 11–31.

"Talk of the Town," *The New Yorker*, February 25, 1967.

PLAYS

The Room, 1957.
The Birthday Party, 1957.
The Dumb Waiter, 1957.
A Slight Ache, 1958 (originally for radio).
A Night Out, 1958 (originally for radio and television).
Night School, 1958 (for television).
"Last to Go" and "Request Stop," sketches for the revue Pieces
    of Eight, 1959.
"The Black and White" and "Trouble in the Works," sketches for
    the revue One to Another, 1959.
The Caretaker, 1959.
The Dwarfs, 1960 (originally for television).
The Collection, 1961 (originally for television).
The Lover, 1964 (originally for television).
The Tea-Party, 1965 (originally for television).
The Homecoming, 1965.
    (In the United States Mr. Pinter is published by Grove Press.
The revue sketches and *The Lover* are also available through The
Dramatists Play Service.)

INTERVIEWS AND ADDITIONAL READING

Bensky, Lawrence M. *Paris Review*, 1967, excerpted in *The New York Times*, January 1, 1967.
Bernhard, F. J. "Beyond Realism: the Plays of Harold Pinter." *Modern Drama*, VIII (1966) 185–91.
Boulton, James T. "Harold Pinter: *The Caretaker* and Other Plays." *Modern Drama*, VI (1964) 131–40.
Bryden, Ronald. "Pinter," *The Observer* (London), February 19, 1967.
Cohn, Ruby. "The World of Harold Pinter." *Tulane Drama Review*, VI (1963) 55–68.
—— "Latter Day Pinter." *Drama Survey*, III (1965) 367–77.
Dukore, Bernard. "The Theatre of Harold Pinter." *Tulane Drama Review*, VI (1963) 43–54.